Lewis Howard Latimer

Published in the United States of America by Cherry Lake Publishing
Ann Arbor, Michigan
www.cherrylakepublishing.com

Content Adviser: Jessica Criales, Doctoral Candidate, History Department, Rutgers University
Reading Adviser: Marla Conn MS, Ed., Literacy specialist, Read-Ability, Inc.
Book Design: Jennifer Wahi
Illustrator: Jeff Bane

Photo Credits: ©Everett Historical/Shutterstock, 5; ©Everett Historical/Shutterstock, 7; ©Burdun Iliya/Shutterstock, 9; ©zoommachine/Shutterstock, 11; ©Joseph Thomas Photography/Shutterstock, 13, 22; ©CC0 1.0 Daderot, 15, 23; ©SIAATH/Shutterstock, 17; ©PD-US War Department, 19; ©PD-US, 21; Cover, 6, 10, 14, Jeff Bane; Various frames throughout, ©Shutterstock Images

Library of Congress Cataloging-in-Publication Data

Names: Marsico, Katie, author.
Title: Lewis Howard Latimer / by Katie Marsico.
Description: Ann Arbor, Michigan : Cherry Lake Publishing, [2018] | Series:
   My itty-bitty bio | Includes bibliographical references and index. |
   Audience: K to grade 3.
Identifiers: LCCN 2018003107| ISBN 9781534128804 (hardcover) | ISBN
   9781534132009 (pbk.) | ISBN 9781534130500 (pdf) | ISBN 9781534133709
   (hosted ebook)
Subjects: LCSH: Latimer, Lewis Howard, 1848-1928--Juvenile literature. |
   African American inventors--Biography--Juvenile literature. |
   Inventors--United States--Biography--Juvenile literature.
Classification: LCC T40.L37 M37 2018 | DDC 609.2 [B] --dc23
LC record available at https://lccn.loc.gov/2018003107

Printed in the United States of America
Corporate Graphics

About the author: Katie Marsico is the author of more than 200 reference books for children and young adults. She lives with her husband and six children near Chicago, Illinois.

About the illustrator: Jeff Bane and his two business partners own a studio along the American River in Folsom, California, home of the 1849 Gold Rush. When Jeff's not sketching or illustrating for clients, he's either swimming or kayaking in the river to relax.

I was born in Massachusetts. My parents were once **slaves** in Virginia.

They ran away. They escaped to the north.

Later, I fought slavery. I served in the Civil War.

Slavery ended after the war.

Next, I worked in a law office.

Inventors often came there.
The **lawyers** made sure no one
stole their ideas.

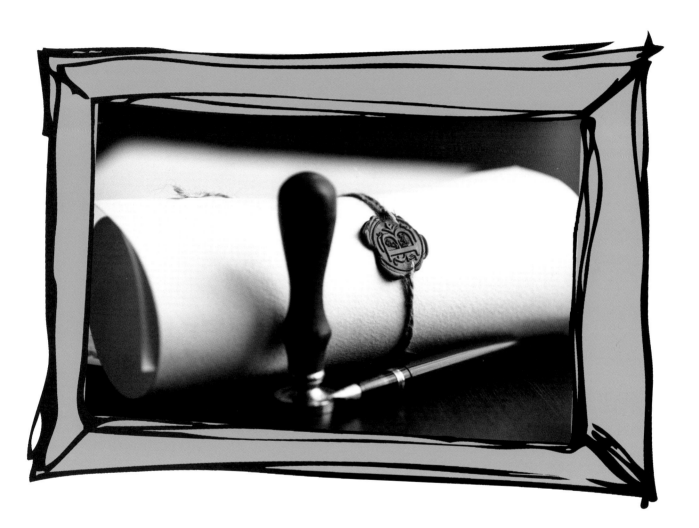

At work, I taught myself to draw.

I was more than an artist, though. I was also an inventor.

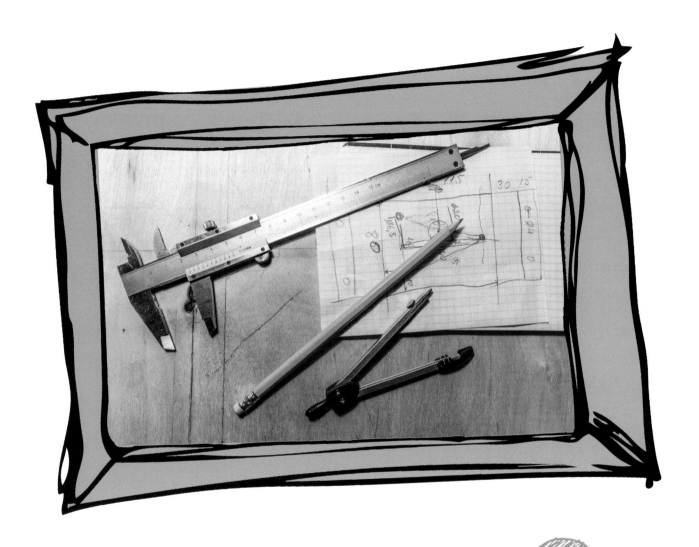

What would you teach yourself?

I improved other people's inventions.

One was the telephone! Another was the **electric** lightbulb.

What would you make better?

I helped bulbs burn longer. My ideas changed electric lighting.

It became easier to light buildings and streets.

Later, I drew a plan for my own elevator. It was safer than earlier ones.

I created an air cleaner.
It cleaned dust from the air.

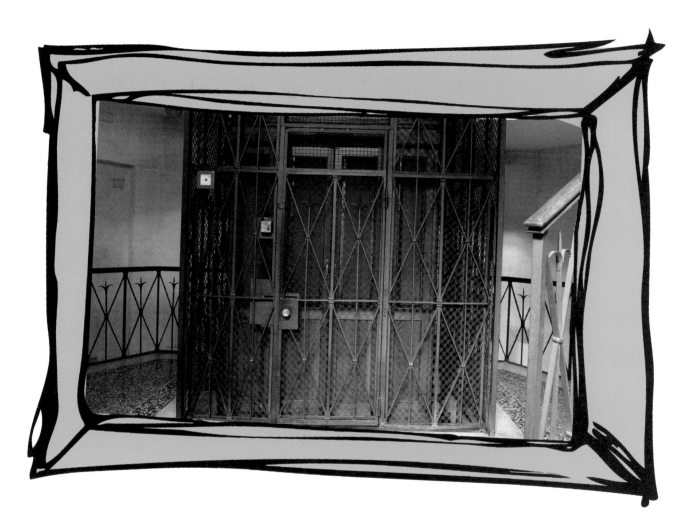

I worked for **equality**, too.
I wanted everyone to know
blacks were Americans.

They should have the same
rights as white Americans.

Why is equality important?

I died in 1928. My career **inspired** others.

I shaped amazing inventions. I showed the world why equality mattered.

What would you like to ask me?

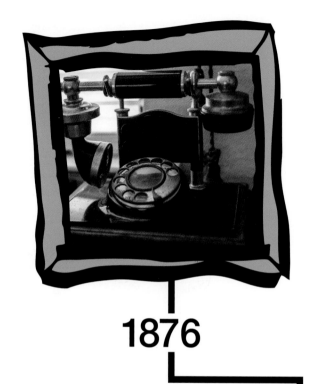

1876

1840

Born
1848

1882

1940

↑
Died
1928

glossary

electric (ih-LEK-trik) powered by a form of energy called electricity

equality (ih-KWAH-lih-tee) the right of everyone to be treated the same

inspired (in-SPYRD) filled someone with a strong feeling or an idea

inventors (in-VEN-turz) people who think up and make something new

lawyers (LOI-urz) people who studied the law and are trained to help others in this matter

slaves (SLAYVZ) people who are owned by other people

index